RE-ENTRY

coming home to a "new normal"

I0081026

Joan Wood

Re-Entry

Coming Home to a "New Normal"

Published by 5 Stones Publishing
First Edition, August 2025

Author Contact: Joan Wood
Email to: joanewood@gmail.com

Publisher Contact:
5 Stones Publishing
Email: Randy2905@gmail.com

ISBN: 978-1-945423-74-1
Printed in the United States of America

A Special Thanks

I would like to thank my grandson, **Joshua Wood**, for the amazing cover of this book. His creativity and keen eye for detail made the design truly perfect. I'm so proud of his work! Joshua, your talent and heart brought this project to life in a way that words alone could never express. Thank you for being part of this journey with me.

Every leader in the body of Christ should read Re-entry. Whether you're a missionary or not, this book is a gift to anyone navigating the realities of the Great Commission. Joan Wood brilliantly equips both short-term and long-term workers with fresh, practical insight while also helping pastors, leaders, and senders better understand their crucial role in the mission.

The Great Commission is best accomplished through collaboration, those who go and those who send, those serving "there" and those supporting "here." Re-entry is the bridge that connects those worlds and will leave you inspired, informed, and better equipped to live and lead with a global Kingdom perspective.

Alex Seidler

Founder and President of The Gateway Project

DEDICATION

This book is dedicated to my one and only Chris Wood, and to our amazing family: Matt & Mary, Hudson, Otis, Ben & Sarah, Isabelle, Joshua, David & Anna, Johanna, Lydia, Emma, and Amelia. You brighten my life with your love!

To my cherished family and friends, thank you for surrounding me with unwavering love and support. You allow me to aim toward being the best reflection of Jesus that I can be, and for that, I am eternally grateful. My prayer is that I give this back, adding blessings in return.

Credit Where Credit Is Due

I would like to thank my friend, **Jack Hempfling**, for writing his book *Before You Go*, which inspired me to write this "bookend" companion on Re-entry. His insights and heart for missionaries helped shape this project in meaningful ways. I am deeply grateful for your wisdom and generosity.

I want to thank my friend, **Randy Johnson**, for gently reminding me of this important question: **Is the Lord calling you to go again?** His words stirred something deep within me, and my final thoughts are shaped by his encouragement.

So I ask you: If you feel that tug to return, to go deeper, or to offer more of yourself for the sake of the Kingdom—don't brush it aside. Sit with it. Pray over it. Talk to wise mentors. Take one faithful step at a time. The call to "go again" may be the beginning of something far greater than you imagined.

Introduction

It is a privilege to take the Good News of Jesus to the people of the earth! I love the colors, cultures, and captivating conversations!

So many precious individuals have not yet heard of the limitless love our amazing God has for them. Jesus commissioned us to go into all the world and preach the Gospel to all creation (Mark 16:15). We "get" to do this, loving like Jesus as we go!

For many years, I have had the honor to be a part of and/or lead teams around the world, bringing Jesus' love in practical and powerful ways. Watching God redeem and transform lives is amazing! God also uses these mission trips to change and transform us, too!

One of the most overlooked dynamics of going is the vital point of coming home. **Re-Entry!** This book is a compilation of practical and reflective thoughts. It is for team leaders preparing their members for the transition, for individuals wrestling with reverse culture shock, and for those at home wanting to support and understand the changes in their loved ones.

To the adventurers: Thank you in advance for going…. and thank you in advance for coming home and being the light and love of Jesus to "your" world and sphere of influence.

May your journey continue even as you **Re-Enter!**

We are on the adventure of Jesus, together!

~joan

Purpose

Every journey has two ends: the leaving and the returning. We celebrate the beginning with excitement and fanfare—commissioning services, prayer gatherings, even airport send-offs filled with hugs and tears. But the return? Too often it slips by quietly, with little attention and even less support. Yet re-entry carries a holy purpose of its own.

Why Re-Entry Matters

Re-Entry has a double aim. First, it creates space for you to reflect, debrief, and find closure for the season you've just lived. Second, it invites you to rediscover your calling here at home—to embrace life in your passport country with fresh perspective and renewed purpose.

This book is written with many people in mind:

- Those arriving home from a short-term mission trip
- Long-term missionaries finishing years of service abroad
- Individuals taking a temporary stay in their passport country
- Ministry workers stepping out of active ministry or into a new role
- Any international worker adjusting back to their home culture

If that describes you, you are not alone.

What Re-Entry Really Is

Re-entry is more than coming back to your street address. It is the process of moving from the culture that became "home" to the one printed in your passport. Many call this

reverse culture shock—and it often feels as disorienting as your very first weeks overseas.

We sometimes expect ourselves—or others—to slide back in effortlessly: put on some jeans, grab a coffee, and get back to normal. But re-entry rarely works that way. For some, "home-sweet-home" feels more like "I want to get on the next plane back."

The Weight of Expectations

And then there are the voices around you:

- "You must be so glad to be back in the 'real' world."
- "We've missed you here – how soon can you jump back in and serve?"
- "When are you going back? Maybe you can lead a group?"
- "Now that you're home, what are you going to do with your life?"

Most people mean well. They want to affirm you. But for someone already walking through exhaustion and disorientation, these questions can feel like heavy weights added to an already full load.

The Heart of Re-Entry

Re-entry is not just about unpacking suitcases. It is about recalibrating your heart and mind to a new reality. It is about discovering how to live with purpose right where God has placed you now. And that process takes time. It won't be finished in a weekend—no matter how many casseroles are waiting at the door.☺

Contents

SECTION 1

ADVENTURES

A CHANGED LIFE

Your life has changed! It will never be the same! You've had new encounters with God and made new friends! You've eaten new foods, and you've experienced new cultures. Lots of new, lots of different... It's amazing how this journey can reshape your life! When Jesus invites us to join Him on an adventure, He shapes and transforms us along the way!

While our original intention for this trip may have been to help others or make the world a better place by sharing the love of Jesus, somewhere along the journey, we ourselves are the ones who are changed.

Some of the changes we experience may include a deepening of our relationship with the Lord, a shift in our perspectives, transformed relationships with others, a broadened worldview, a renewed sense of purpose and mission, and a greater appreciation for different cultures.

An impactful trip can cause internal tensions between how we used to think...and how we think now. This takes time to process and articulate.

Upon **re-entry**, it can be incredibly difficult to put these changes into words. We come home with fresh emotions and deep experiences that are hard to fully express. People will ask, 'How was your trip?'—But how do you sum up something that changed your heart in just a few sentences? We will talk about this in a later section.

It's a harder transition coming back from the mission field than going...because you've been changed more than you know.

You set out on the adventure, having a blast with a team of like-minded people who had a purpose and mission to accomplish:

> *Psalm 96:3 "Declare His glory among the nations, His wonders among all peoples."*

And now you're back to work, your routines, making meals, doing the dishes, does laundry ever stop?

Ho Hummmm...

You may ask yourself, "What am I doing with my life?" "Am I making a difference here at home?" I'm just back to the "same old, same old"! You may even feel guilty, thinking, "I have so much, and they have so little." "I want to do more." You don't usually walk away from a trip unchanged...

Take a moment to reflect and consider how you've changed. Jot your thought here:

You don't usually walk away from a trip unchanged!

Somewhere along the way in my adventures with Jesus, He changed my perspectives on life, and I'd like to share them with you. ☺

BE A PILGRIM

Pilgrim, traveler, nomad, wanderer - All words to denote a person on a journey or adventure. I like to think of my life with Jesus as an adventure.

One thing I have discovered about this adventure, God doesn't usually send me a rigid itinerary, with all the stops mapped out, but instead, **it's an invitation to be with Him.** God knows me so well: I think if I knew the destination, I would try to beat Him there! ☺

Every day, I start from a place of gratitude for His faithfulness and limitless love for me. It's the solid ground to stand on! He promises never to leave me, so I won't have to journey alone. He promises His goodness and mercy to follow me, so He's got my back covered! And He promises that I will have lots of joy and pleasure in His presence!

> *Psalm 16:11 "You will show me the path of life; In Your presence is fullness of joy; At Your right hand are pleasures forevermore."*

God's promises are always true, so I'm going to enjoy this adventure with Him! This is the verse that started me on this idea of being a pilgrim:

> *Psalm 84:5,6 "Blessed is the man whose strength is in You, whose heart is set on pilgrimage. As they pass through the Valley of Baca, they make it a spring."*

Finding our daily strength in the Lord is key to our journey and pilgrimage with Jesus. On a trip, it is easy; we have daily devotions, daily prayer, and daily Bible reading with our mission community. Team members also encourage each other with lots of "God-thoughts" throughout the day!

One of the challenges of re-entry and being back at home is following through on the **daily** God-part of life. Life happens! We may not be surrounded by other Jesus followers…our circle has changed. Or we're back to work, and our daily schedule is crazier than when we left! It takes work to tame our daily schedules!

> *Finding our DAILY strength in the Lord is key to our journey!*

Continuing in these verses, as we set our hearts on a pilgrimage or adventure with the Lord Jesus, and allow Him to be our life and strength, then we become ambassadors for Him.

The Valley of Baca was a place of sorrow or hard times. The verse states that when we pass through the places of sorrow or hard times, we make those places better by bringing Jesus to them! We become ambassadors of joy, hope, and love!

Places of sorrow or hard times are not only in the villages of Africa, they may also be next door to us or happening in our co-worker's life. Consider a single parent working multiple jobs, or a student overwhelmed by expectations, or a friend quietly struggling with anxiety or depression. As we find our life and strength in Jesus, we have something wonderful to share with them to help them through the tough times- Jesus! Every place our feet step, we can bring the light and love and hope and joy of Jesus and make it a better place, as the verse says, a spring!

I like to keep Psalm 84:5-7 as my life vision & mission. This is what I call having a "Pilgrim's Worldview." My heart is always open for another adventure with Jesus, even if it happens at the grocery store!

> *Proverbs 29:18 "Where there is no vision, the people perish..."*

Is your heart ready for another adventure with Jesus, even at the grocery store?

Take a moment to encourage yourself in the Lord with some promises in God's word that will strengthen you. Write a couple of your favorites here:

"Is there someone in your life who might be going through a tough or dry season? What would it look like to encourage them in a practical, meaningful way?"

What does having a Pilgrim's Worldview mean to you?

CONFIRMING
OUR CITIZENSHIP

To ease the challenges of **Re-Entry**, confirm your citizenship in heaven. When you're on the move with God, the scenery changes. From the vast expanse of the Amazon River to the majestic heights of the Himalayas, God's creation houses His people. Our citizenship in heaven establishes Kingdom of God priorities in our lives and keeps us on mission even when the landscape of our lives shifts. As citizens of heaven, we live on earth with a daily passion, fervent here or abroad, serving others and reflecting Christ wherever we are.

Take a moment to consider these verses:

Philippians 3:20 The Message: "But there's far more to life for us. We're citizens of high heaven! We're waiting for the arrival of the Savior, the Master, Jesus Christ, who will transform our earthly bodies into glorious bodies like his own. He'll make us beautiful and whole with the same powerful skill by which he is putting everything as it should be, under and around him."

1 Peter 2:11 The Message "Friends, this world is not your home, so don't make yourselves cozy in it. Don't indulge your ego at the expense of your soul. Live an exemplary life in your neighborhood so that your actions will refute their prejudices. Then they'll be won over to God's side and be there to join in the celebration when he arrives".

> ## Drop the word 'HOME' from your vocabulary; you're just changing mission fields!

Sometimes, the word **"home"** can evoke feelings of comfort, familiarity, and routine. But with that comfort can come complacency — a tendency to let our guard down, grow spiritually passive, or forget the **mission and purpose** that God has called us to. Coming back to familiar settings can cause us to lose our dependency on God or our hunger for His Word.

On a trip, we often shift our mindset. We're alert. We're ready. We step out of our comfort zones and say, **"Here I am, Lord — use me in any way."** We serve with open hands and willing hearts, often in unfamiliar places or roles. For example, clean toilets, dig a trench, carry ridiculously heavy equipment from one place to another,☺ but how about at home?

Here's the truth: **that same spirit of availability, humility, and purpose is just as needed at home —** maybe even more so. God doesn't only call us on mission trips. He calls us in the classroom, at our jobs, in our families, and with our friends. You may love working with kids on a trip, but are you volunteering for the nursery or teaching Sunday School in your home church? Hmmmm.

Don't let "home" become an excuse for spiritual laziness. Let it be the place where your mission truly begins.

> ## Home is the place where your mission truly begins!

Take a moment to consider these verses:

> *1 Corinthians 10:31 NKJV "Therefore, whether you eat or drink, or whatever you do, do all to the glory of God."*

> *Colossians 3:17,23 NKJV "And whatever you do in word or deed, do all in the name of the Lord Jesus, giving thanks to God the Father through Him. Vs 23 And whatever you do, do it heartily, as to the Lord and not to men."*

A few more verses for you to think about: Take a minute and journal what they mean to you.

> *Ephesians 2:19 NKJV "Now, therefore, you are no longer strangers and foreigners, but fellow citizens with the saints and members of the household of God."*

> *Hebrews 11:13 NIV "All these people were still living by faith when they died. They did not receive the things promised; they only saw them and welcomed them from a distance, admitting that they were foreigners and strangers on earth."*

Philippians 3:20 "For our citizenship is in heaven, from which we also eagerly wait for the Savior, the Lord Jesus Christ."

When we become citizens of heaven, we are enlisted in God's army, advancing the Kingdom of heaven here on earth. In my limited understanding of our military system, I believe that when you join the U.S. military, you agree to live by a different set of laws, and you agree to uphold a higher standard of discipline, loyalty, and obedience.

> **To minimize the effects of re-entry, confirm your citizenship in heaven, and maximize your residence on earth.**

Similarly, as **citizens of God's Kingdom, we are called to live by a new set of values – Kingdom values**. We no longer live according to the patterns of this world, but we live under the authority of our King Jesus. Our mission is clear: to love God, love people, and make disciples. We are to bring light into darkness and hope into broken places.

Just like the military, there is sacrifice, training, and battle – but the victory is already won through Christ!

We no longer live for ourselves, but for the cause of Christ. We are His ambassadors, bringing His love to a world that desperately needs Him.

What do these thoughts mean to you, practically?

When we stop living for ourselves and live for the cause of Christ, what does that mean to you?

What are the benefits of being a citizen of heaven?

Write some thoughts about "home" being the place where your mission begins.

Defining The Mission

To quote an old movie, "Our mission, should we choose to accept it", is to spread the Good News of Jesus everywhere we go! Is that what you did on the mission trip? Then that's what He wants you to do at home, too! Simple!

Just the address of the mission has changed; instead of Ethiopia/ Kenya/ Thailand, etc., it's now Hometown, your passport country!

God has us exactly where He wants us. We were born to specific parents, and we live in specific places. If you were supposed to be born in Africa, you would have been! God has a reason, a purpose, and a mission for your life and mine.

The mission is the same; only the address has changed!

Take a minute and journal your thoughts about your mission. Put it in your own words and keep it simple!

Team Dynamics

As I stated before, you've been having a blast with a team of like-minded people who have a purpose and a mission to accomplish. This has created a sense of community. An important dynamic of this community is that you've been working together, championing one another and each other's gifts and talents…all to exalt and glorify God!

> **God brings diverse people together to accomplish His purposes!**

This is practically worked out as we identify our own weaknesses, understanding that we can't do it all or alone. Weakness is not a bad thing; it encourages us to work together as a body or team. We don't focus on our differences but appreciate one another, recognizing how God has brought so many diverse people together to accomplish His purpose. Embracing this truth enhances team dynamics.

You bring your own strengths and weaknesses to the team dynamics, and so do the others. As we work together in a team, our potential to accomplish God's purpose is multiplied exponentially and God is glorified!

> **If you want to go fast, go alone. If you want to go far, go together.**

This African proverb emphasizes the importance of collaboration and teamwork in achieving ambitious goals, suggesting that while individual efforts can be efficient, working with others allows for greater progress and impact over time. It's often used to encourage people to consider the long-term benefits of cooperation and community building.

Consider the Ice Cream Cone

Did you know that the Ice Cream Cone was invented at the World's Fair in St Louis in 1904 when an ice cream vendor ran out of bowls, and a nearby waffle maker saved the day!

This fun fact illustrates the idea that working together can even bring new, innovative, and creative solutions.

You may be the solution to someone else's problem!

Consider these Scriptures and write down some of your strengths and weaknesses:

> I Corinthians 12:20-22 "But now indeed there are many members, yet one body. And the eye cannot say to the hand, "I have no need of you"; nor again the head to the feet, "I have no need of you." No, much rather, those members of the body which seem to be weaker are necessary."

Ecclesiastes 4:9 "Two are better than one, because they have a good return for their labor."

Philippians 2:1-4 NLT "Is there any encouragement from belonging to Christ? Any comfort from his love? Any fellowship together in the Spirit? Are your hearts tender and compassionate? ² Then make me truly happy by agreeing wholeheartedly with each other, loving one another, and working together with one mind and purpose.³ Don't be selfish; don't try to impress others. Be humble, thinking of others as better than yourselves. ⁴ Don't look out only for your own interests, but take an interest in others, too."

How can you help others today?

How can you become more aware of others' needs around you?

Are you more comfortable going it alone? If so, pause and reflect on how working together might be more beneficial.

What is one gift/talent that the Lord has given you that might blend with someone else?

COMMUNITY

Community is HUGE! You've been planning this trip with a group of people for a long time! They have become your "family" for a little while. Friendships were forged in unexpected places, and when the tough times came, there was always someone there to spur you on and pray with you! I love this dynamic of team building on a mission!

Friendships formed in a common place and time, and through shared experiences, can last a lifetime. I believe friendships are God's idea. Jesus calls us friends! To have a friend, you must be a friend! Cherish and treasure the friendships that you make on your journey.

> *John 15:15 "No longer do I call you servants, for a servant does not know what his master is doing; but I have called you friends, for all things that I heard from My Father I have made known to you."*

Community is also created and sustained by loving and serving one another. On a trip, you will have multiple opportunities to think of others before yourself and serve them. This is what Jesus did for us!

> *I John 4:11 "Beloved, if God so loved us, we also ought to love one another."*

**Friendship is God's idea!
Jesus calls us friends.**

I believe, one of the greatest treasures in the Kingdom of God is friendship. How we treat and serve one another displays the gift of friendship.

> *John 15:13 "Greater love has no one than this, than to lay down one's life for his friends."*

Consider the Cow....

Fun Fact: Cows have best friends. Cows form close bonds and often have best friends within their herds. These social animals can become stressed when separated from their companions.

What new friendships have you made?

What are your thoughts on friendship?

What does it mean to be a friend?

How is Jesus a friend to you?

Who are your friends here at home? How can you serve them?

Loss of Community

Sometimes, upon returning, you may feel lonely and miss your "mission's family." Home can often make you feel isolated, as you've lost your day-to-day community of encouragers. Reach out! Text someone on the team! Stay in contact with them.

Being part of a greater mission brings a secure sense of belonging. You can laugh about the shared experiences you had while on the trip. They were there; you don't have to explain! Call a friend for a cup of tea! Don't fall into the trap of isolation. Discouragement and depression are real! Reach out! Stay in community.

> ## Reach Out!

Loss of purpose adds to the feelings of isolation and separation from the community. Some of the effects of isolation can lead to mental health issues, anxiety, depression, feelings of resentment toward people, drug or alcohol abuse, and further anti-social behavior.

If you're feeling discouraged or isolated, identify it, acknowledge it, and stay vigilant. If you are feeling depressed or lonely, remember that one of your team members may feel the same—reach out and support them by checking in on them.

Remember the Cow: they often feel stressed when separated.

> ## Phone a Friend!

What practical things can you do to stay connected to a community?

Some friendships are just for a season. If your "mission community" is far away, who is your new community?

Be A Barnabas

Acts 4:36 NIV "Joseph, a Levite from Cyprus, whom the apostles called Barnabas (which means 'son of encouragement')."

You've consistently been a source of encouragement for team members over the past few weeks. Even in moments when it might have been easier to step away, you chose to uplift others and keep momentum going. Barnabas's example of encouragement affected many and kept the Kingdom of God advancing!

Acts 11:22-24 "...and they sent out Barnabas to go as far as Antioch. When he came and had seen the grace of God, he was glad and encouraged them all that with purpose of heart they should continue with the Lord. For he was a good man, full of the Holy Spirit and of faith. And a great many people were added to the Lord."

On our trip, we embraced the values of **Edify, Praise, and Honor.** These guiding principles shaped how we treated one another, spoke life into our surroundings, and built a stronger, more uplifting community.

**Edify with your words.
Praise what is good.
Honor others with your actions.**

Now that we're home, it's essential to **remember, adopt, and actively live out these values** in our everyday lives. Let the same spirit of encouragement, affirmation, and respect guide your words and actions — not just on special trips, but at school, at home, with friends, and in every interaction.

Keep the encouragement going — because these values don't just belong to the trip, they belong to the life you're building at home.

Edify, Praise & Honor

Edify is an architectural term meaning to fortify, construct, and build up. You and I were designed by God to fortify and build others up. He gave us particular God- given gifts to encourage others around us. When the Jerusalem church sent Barnabas to encourage the Antioch believers, the kingdom of God flourished. (Acts 11:22)

A thought of praise unspoken is a blessing left ungiven!

Praise means to verbally approve, commend, or applaud. Words are important and powerful! **Spoken praise carries weight** that internal thoughts alone cannot match.

When we take the time to **express our appreciation out loud**, we're not only affirming someone else's value — we're also building trust, deepening relationships, and creating a positive atmosphere around us. Words, when used with intention, can **uplift, inspire, and even transform** a person's day or outlook.

So next time you admire someone's kindness, effort, or growth — **Say it. Speak it. Share it.** You never know how much someone may need to hear those encouraging words.

On one of our trips, I overheard my daughter bragging on me, and it really moved my heart. God's heart is also moved when we brag on Him, what He's done, how we've seen Him work in our lives and the lives of others!   Take every opportunity to praise God and praise those around you!

> Psalm 145:3 *"Great is the LORD, and greatly to be praised; And His greatness is unsearchable. One generation shall praise Your works to another and shall declare Your mighty acts. I will meditate on the glorious splendor of Your majesty, and on Your wondrous works. Men shall speak of the might of Your awesome acts, And I will declare Your greatness."*

Honor denotes high respect, esteem, credit, kudos. Creating a culture of honor in our everyday life is so important to our success when returning home from a mission trip. Honoring others is key to living a life of selflessness.

Just plan on being nice... Forever!

> Philippians 2:3,4 *" Let nothing be done through selfish ambition or conceit, but in lowliness of mind let each esteem others better than himself. Let each of you look out not only for his own interests, but also for the interests of others."*

On this trip, there may have been times when you thought of others before you thought of yourself. Don't go back to selfishness! Thinking of others and being selfless is a practical way to demonstrate Christ every day. Just plan on being nice...forever!

Thoughts to ponder...Hmmm

When John Mark was rejected because of a perceived failure - Barnabas gave him a second chance. John Mark ended up writing the Gospel of Mark.

What might have happened had Barnabas not encouraged him?

Who can you edify today?

What words of affirmation can you encourage someone with today?

What are some ways to honor others around you?

Just be nice…forever! What does that mean to you? Is there anything you are currently doing that needs to change?

Consider the Dolphin….

Fun Fact: Dolphins have names for each other. They have a signature whistle to identify themselves and use these whistles to call to one another.

Let's look again at Barnabas. According to Acts 4, his given name was Joseph of Cyprus, but the apostles started calling him Barnabas, which means son of encouragement. They changed his name because of how he lived his life, always encouraging others. This tells us a lot about Barnabas' character and who he was among them – a constant encourager! This is significant because in Biblical times, names often reflected identity and calling.

Cheer loudly for others!

Names are important. Jesus called Peter by a new name, denoting his destiny in God. John (one of the "sons of thunder") had his name changed to "beloved one". What changed?

Is there a not -so- nice name you've been called? Is it possible to change? How?

Nicknames are fun when they encourage or uplift others. Think of some of your friends, how could you encourage them with a new nickname?

Sunny Sally, Joyful Janet, Gracious Gary, Helpful Henry.

Judgments & Contentment

One of the hidden dangers of re-entry is how easily we can become judgmental. It often starts small- maybe. Just a thought like, "Americans are so spoiled…"—and before long it hardens into an attitude. The very things that used to feel normal suddenly get under our skin.

Re-entry doesn't just shake up our routines; it uncovers what's going on in our hearts. And it gently reminds us that grace wasn't only something we needed "out there" on the field—we need it just as much right here at home.

After spending time in places marked by poverty or spiritual darkness, we may come back with a subtle sense of superiority: "We've seen real need. We know what sacrifice is." Or we catch ourselves complaining: "Why is the church spending on carpet when some people don't have food?"

But let's be honest—that isn't humility. It's pride, disguised as compassion. Paul points us to a better way in Philippians.

> *Philippians 4:10-14 " I rejoiced greatly in the Lord that at last you renewed your concern for me. Indeed, you were concerned, but you had no opportunity to show it.[11] I am not saying this because I am in need, for I have learned to be content whatever the circumstances. [12] I know what it is to be in need, and I know what it is to have plenty. I have learned the secret of being*

*content in any and every situation, whether
well fed or hungry, whether living in plenty or in
want. ¹³ I can do all this through him who gives
me strength.¹⁴ Yet it was good of you to share in
my troubles."*

Heart Check:

- Am I extending the same grace at home that I so freely offered overseas?
- How might Jesus be inviting me to see my home culture through His eyes of compassion?
- What would it look like today to choose gratitude instead of criticism?
- Who in my life needs to see me respond with humility and love rather than judgment?

We didn't go to elevate ourselves — we went to serve, to love, and to see people through God's eyes. Yes, there is a stark contrast between our material abundance at home and the physical poverty we witnessed. But the real difference is not about wealth — **it's about identity and contentment in God.**

In many parts of the world, people often don't comprehend the truth that they are created in the image of God, and that in Christ, we have all we need.

When people are unaware that they bear God's image, it impacts how they see themselves and how they treat others. As we serve and encourage others around the world, we bring more than just food or medical services— we carry with us the **truth of their worth and the solid reality of God's faithfulness.**

We also had the joy of serving across denominations, united not by every doctrine, but by one unshakable foundation: We exalted Jesus above all else.

Let's carry that same spirit home:

- No judgment.
- No spiritual pride.
- Just a deep love for God and His children.

We exalt Jesus above all else!

Do you have an issue with being judgmental? If so, confess it to the Lord, repent, and ask Him to help you see people through His eyes and with His heart.

How can you practice seeing people through God's eyes and with His heart?

How does knowing your identity in Christ shape the way you see yourself?

Meditate on the faithfulness of God to you personally. Write about your feelings of contentment.

ATTITUDE OF GRATITUDE

Psalm 136:1 "Give thanks to the Lord, for He is good. His love endures forever."

One of the best ways to overcome some of the pitfalls of **Re-Entry** is to cultivate an attitude of gratitude! When I stop and think about the blessing and privilege we've just experienced—traveling to a different place and spending time with such a unique people group—I'm overwhelmed with gratitude and my heart responds with, 'We get to do this'!

Try these prayers of gratitude:

- "Lord, thank You for letting me take care of some of Your children."

- "Lord, thank You for supplying all my needs."

- "Lord, thank You for being such a creative God that the entire world is Your masterpiece."

- "Lord, thank You for Your protection and care over me as I traveled."

- "Lord, thank You for filling my heart with love for others."

- "Lord, thank You for new friends around the world."

Write a couple of your own.

Tips for Testimonies

Your life has changed! It will never be the same! You've had fresh experiences with God and made new friends! You've eaten unique foods, you've experienced unfamiliar cultures, and it's hard to put all of the raw emotions and feelings into words when you get home. My suggestion is to keep your answers short and sweet. **It's virtually impossible to recreate the sights, sounds, smells, and tastes of another country!**

I also recommend that you take advantage of the time on your flight home to write down a couple of stories that you may want to share. Prepare a 30-second synopsis of your trip! This will take some thought and preparation. You might even want to practice it on the person sitting next to you!

People will ask, "How was your trip?

My go-to first answer to that question is always, 'Great!' Then I pause to see if they want to know more. If they do, I don't give them the whole movie—I give them the poster. Just a 20-second story about something that truly touched my heart. Enough to connect, not overwhelm. Most people are satisfied with just that. People love hearing how your heart has been touched—it makes the moment real. Most of the time, that's enough. It satisfies curiosity while still keeping things personal and meaningful.

Don't give them the movie, give them the poster!

Identify the audience

When giving your testimony It is important stay aware of who is asking the question. Your audience will often shape your response.

1st Audience: Most people want it simple and sweet!

2nd Audience: If the person asking is a family member or friend, you can give them the poster version plus a couple more stories. Try to keep your stories concise and highlight the meaningful parts. Avoid minute-by-minute replays!

Short and Sweet!

Here are some suggestions:

- "Wow, it feels like ages since we last talked! I miss you!"   (Share a quick overview, then a few meaningful stories — imagine these like highlights on a movie poster.)
- "One of the most amazing things I got to experience was…"
- "I had this incredible moment where…" (insert a highlight: something you accomplished, or something unexpected that taught you a lot)
- "One experience that really touched me was…"
- "Something that really changed how I see things happened when…" (share a more emotional or personal moment, even if it was small — something that changed how you see things)
- "And then there was this funny/random thing…" (a light-hearted or weird story for balance)
- "But I want to hear about *you* too — what's been going on in your world?"
- "What's something that's made you laugh recently? Or something that's been on your mind?"

3rd Audience: Your spouse or very close friend. They will probably want more details. Don't try to tell them the entire trip on your first day home; spread out the stories. Try not to get offended if they fall asleep during the minute-by-minute replays! ☺

My friend, **Todd Fowler**, shared a few tips with me regarding the ones who stayed home to "hold down the fort." They, too, have been having different experiences during the time that you were away. Ask them what has been going on in their lives as well. Give them a chance to talk, too! And try not to fall asleep while they're talking! ☺

Give them a chance to talk, too!

Two more testimony tips:

- **Always point people to our amazing God**—give Him all the glory and praise for what He has done in your life and in the lives of others.

- A great template to help you organize your thoughts: **Eye, Heart, Hand**. I saw something, I felt something, and I did something.

    The **"why" of our trip** is rooted in Jesus' example: He saw the crowds, was moved with compassion, healed the sick, and fed the hungry.

Eye – Heart – Hand

Take a few minutes and write down a short testimony using the template above: Eye, Heart, Hand. (on next page)

Questions to consider when writing your testimony:

- Who were the people?
- Where did you go?

- What did you do?
- Scripture thought?
- How was I changed?
- How was God glorified?
- What was something you learned?
- What did you see God do?

Your Testimony:

_____

_____

_____

_____

_____

_____

_____

_____

_____

_____

_____

_____

Thanks & Updates

Remember to thank your supporters! Your home team – those who prayed faithfully and those who gave generously – who were a vital part of your journey.

They are eager to hear how God worked during your trip. Create a one-page newsletter to update them. Share a story or moment that impacted you. Include several pictures of people, places, and YOU in action! Keep it brief and meaningful!

Personal thank-you notes are also a great way to express your appreciation. Practicing your attitude of gratitude helps your **Re-Entry** process.

Take a minute and jot down a couple of thoughts you can use when you write thank-you notes and a newsletter.

_____

_____

_____

_____

_____

_____

_____

_____

PILGRIM WORLDVIEW POINTERS

Here are some quick thoughts on living as a pilgrim in our everyday world. Pilgrim's don't wander aimlessly. Our worldview can be guided by these values. We meet strangers everyday and being prepared enables us to see them as fellow travelers and treat them as Jesus would.

Cultural Issues

- Cultural flexibility refers to the ability to adapt effectively and appropriately to different cultures.
- Have a willingness to accept and learn from different perspectives without judgment.
- Observe and ask questions without judgment.
- Have the understanding that people from different backgrounds may approach situations in unique ways according to their culture.
- Have empathy by putting yourself in someone else's "shoes" to understand their reactions and behaviors better.
- Be willing to adjust your language, tone and body language to ensure communication is effectively conveyed and received.

Be Alert

- Have all 5 senses on alert.
- Listen to their language.
- Be aware of acceptable "dress".
- Be perceptive: nothing is insignificant.

- Ask for increased discernment as to what is essential.
- Be aware of distractions and identify them, so as not to be derailed from your goals.
- Don't take things for granted. Small things are important!
    - safe travels: like the car working...no flat tires☺
    - health
    - divine appointments
- Always remember to have an attitude of gratitude!

Serving

This is a quote from "Gingerbrook Fare", a children's ministry - 1980's **"Cheerfully doing what I'm asked to do; and doing it quickly because I love you."**

- Have a willingness to serve in any capacity.
- Have the heart posture of doing all in service to the Lord.

   Isaiah 49:6 *"Is it such a small thing to be a servant of the Most High God?"*

Lasting Changes

- Live daily with a passion as fervent as on the mission trip.
- Be nice...forever!
- Resist the pull of selfishness. Living selflessly is a practical and powerful way to reflect the character of Christ in everyday life.
- Cheer loudly for others.

> **Home is the place where your mission truly begins.**

Actionable Advice

When you return home, it's normal to experience some practical challenges such as tummy issues, jet lag or disrupted sleep. The following simple tips are offered to help you navigate these issues and others.

Tummy Issues

On most mission trips, you've been eating different foods. Give your body time to adjust.

Coming back from a mission trip usually means your diet changes again—and your body might feel it! It's pretty normal to have some indigestion, loose bowels, or even constipation as you get back to your usual eating habits.

If things don't settle down, check in with your team leader—they may have some helpful tips. And if it lasts more than a week, it's a good idea to see your doctor and let them know you've been overseas.

Jet Lag

Don't be a grump in the afternoon slump!

Drink Water...Water...and more water! Water really helps your body acclimate on many different levels. Jet lag is real—be patient with yourself!

Traveling across time zones can really throw off your sleep. You might find yourself wide awake at 4 AM and struggling to stay awake by mid-afternoon.

The best thing you can do? Try to stay awake during the day (especially in the afternoon) and head to bed a little earlier than usual for a few days. Your body will adjust—just give it some grace and time! Remember, don't be a grump in the afternoon slump!

Disorientation & Confusion

You might catch yourself thinking, "I'm home…but it doesn't feel like home." If that's you, you're not alone. Almost everyone who walks through re-entry feels this way at some point. The place hasn't changed much—but you have. And that's why things don't feel the same.

It takes time to figure out what home looks like now and to settle into your "new normal." One missionary laughed as they admitted, "I've got all these big, life-changing decisions to make…and I can't even decide what kind of bread to buy. There are too many choices!"

That's re-entry for you. It sneaks up in the serious moments…and even in the bread aisle.

So here's the best thing you can do: take a breath. Slow down. Spend some quiet time with the Lord. And when you think you've had enough, give yourself a little more. The world can wait—it really can. Right now, your soul needs space.

> *Proverbs 16:9 "A man's heart plans his way, But the Lord directs his steps."*
>
> *Psalm 27:14 "Wait on the Lord; Be of good courage, And He shall strengthen your heart; Wait, I say, on the Lord!"*

Slow down

Purposely schedule some quiet time, to slow down, at least a day or two.

- Don't hit the ground running!

- Busyness is not your friend right now.
- Reflect, Rest & Reconnect with God.

Swelling

- If you have some swelling in your legs, feet or ankles, drinking lots of water will help immensely!
- Stay away from Soda/Pop, most have a lot of sodium, which will keep your ankles and feet swollen.
- Also, get up and walk!

Sleep

It takes a bit of time to adjust back to your normal sleep patterns. However, if you do wake early, take advantage of this time and be productive. Extra time in the early hours of the day is sweet when spent with Jesus and His Word.

> *Psalm 63:1 "O God, You are my God; Early will I seek You; My soul thirsts for You; My flesh longs for You In a dry and thirsty land Where there is no water."*

While you're awake, you can always spend some time praying for your team members. They're probably awake praying for you!☺

Tips for Leaders

Being a leader is a big responsibility, but it is also an opportunity to set the tone for the group. One way to do this is by creating moments of fun and camaraderie along the journey. Remember it's laughter and shared stories that help create life long memories and friendships.

Sing complaints

One of the best tips for maintaining a positive team attitude is to bring in humor. At some point in every trip, there are reasons to complain. Hot, cold, tired, cranky, hungry, sore, _____fill in the blank!

One of my favorite rules is that if you MUST complain, do it in an operatic singing voice! Try it sometime...You can't keep complaining if you're singing like an opera star! Everyone busts out laughing!

Sing your complaints like an opera singer!

Thinking of others

A fun thing I do when packing for my trip is to ask the Lord, "What could I pack that someone else may need?" And then watch for the time that it is needed...It makes me smile that God is concerned about even the smallest detail of our lives and that we get to partner with Him!

Suggest this to your team when you're giving them packing tips.

Community

A practical idea: Get the team back together for a meal and try to make some of the different foods you ate while on the mission's trip. But have a pizza place ready just in case the ethnic food is a bust! ☺

Be A Barnabas

Nicknames: Joseph of Cyprus gets a nickname. What's yours?

Take time to pray for each team member and ask the Lord to show you something special about each one. Throughout your trip, look for times when this "nickname" is demonstrated.

- Look for opportunities to highlight that name during the trip. For example: If you see someone has a "sunny" or cheerful disposition, you might greet them in the morning and say, "Good morning, Sunshine." Or during the week, say, "Hey Sunshine".

- At the debrief meeting with your team, you can highlight each team member with their (positive) nickname and cite some of the ways you saw it demonstrated. They will remember that for a long time…

Encourage team members to continue this at home.☺

SECTION 2

EXTENDED ADVENTURES

Longer journeys often change us in ways we don't fully see until we return home. The experiences are rich, the challenges more complex, and re-entry can be a bit trickier. The thoughts and insights that follow are offered to guide you through both the journey and the return, helping you navigate growth, change, and make the most of the road ahead.

CHANGE

Re-entry is never just about geography. It's about the shock of realizing that the world you're stepping back into isn't quite the one you left—and that you're not quite the same person either. Coming home means facing changes both around you and within you. Recognizing them is the first step toward adjusting with grace.

Shifts Around You

- **Church & Community:** You may walk into your sending church and discover a new pastor, a different leadership team, or even a whole generation of faces you don't recognize. Maybe people you loved have moved on—or even moved away.
- **Cultural Climate:** Political debates may be raging over issues that didn't exist when you left. Social values can shift quickly, leaving you feeling like the conversations have changed mid-sentence.
- **Family Life:** Weddings, divorces, births, illnesses—life has gone on in your absence. You may find yourself grieving moments you never got to witness.
- **Everyday Norms:** Technology and trends move fast. You may feel out of place when everyone pays with their phone, menus are only available by QR code, or our children's classmates talk about apps you've never heard of.

Shifts Within You

- **Body & Health:** Mission life takes a toll. You may notice the aches, the fatigue, or the simple fact of feeling older than when you left.

- **Relationships & Roles:** Maybe your marital status has changed. Maybe your children are older now, carrying responsibilities you never imagined when you first left. Perhaps you carry new ministry experiences that have reshaped how you relate to others.

- **Spiritual & Emotional Growth:** You've prayed in the dark, cried through disappointments, and celebrated breakthroughs. You may come home with a deeper faith, greater endurance, and a sharper compassion.

- **Identity & Perspective:** After years of living between worlds, you may feel caught between cultures. Your values, tastes, and worldview have stretched. You may feel more at home abroad than in your own passport country. Yet, in Christ, you are anchored—and that identity remains unshaken.

Friend, don't be surprised by these changes. Don't even resent them. Instead, receive them as signs that God has been shaping you—and that He isn't finished yet.

ADJUSTMENT

Adjustment is not a weekend project. Coming home takes time—longer than most of us want to admit. Counselors who walk with missionaries often say that transition can stretch out over years, not weeks. Whether it takes one, two, or even three years, the point is this: be patient with yourself. Give your heart a long runway to land.

Without preparation and care, the weight of unprocessed emotions can quietly build until they show up as discouragement, burnout, or bitterness. But with awareness, you can meet this season with grace instead of frustration.

Traveling lightly is not what is in your suitcase—it's about what you carry in your heart and mind. **Re-Entry** stress can seem even greater when you feel misunderstood, out of place, or unsupported. To lighten the load, identify and reflect on these instinctively common—but ultimately unhelpful—responses.

Unhelpful Ways We Often Respond

It's natural to stumble into unhealthy patterns as we try to cope with change. See if any of these sound familiar:

- **The Silent Struggle:** You pull inward, choosing not to share, hoping someone will just "get it" without you saying a word.
- **The Critic's Chair:** You find yourself pointing out what's wrong with your home culture—sometimes with sharp words, sometimes with quiet disdain.
- **The Endless Comparison:** You measure everything against "back there," always finding home lacking.

- **Glossing It Over:** You tell everyone you're fine, smile through the gatherings, and push down the ache.
- **The Golden Filter:** You remember the past through rose-colored glasses, forgetting that the field had its own hardships too.
- **Blame and Distance:** You assume others don't understand—and that it's their fault. That keeps you feeling isolated, even from those who want to care.

Meeting Anger and Pain With Christ

The good news is: Christ is not distant from these emotions. He Himself felt anger at sin and injustice. He wept with grief over loss. On the cross, He bore the deepest pain of all—abandonment, betrayal, and suffering. Because of this, He not only understands our emotions, but He welcomes us to bring them to Him.

When anger rises, instead of burying it or letting it spill out on others, we can bring it honestly to Christ. When pain feels overwhelming, we can let Him hold it with us. In His presence, anger can be transformed into righteous passion, and pain can become a doorway to deeper dependence on Him.

Meeting our anger and pain with Christ doesn't mean ignoring or minimizing them—it means inviting Him to meet us in those places with His healing, peace, and perspective.

At some point, every returnee faces anger, loss, pain or grief. When those moments come, you stand at a crossroads. One path leads to Jesus (peace, forgiveness & wholeness)—the other leads to bitterness and toxic life patterns.

- **The Path of Surrender:** Bring your pain into the light of Christ. Name it honestly. In the Christian faith, naming your pain is not a sign of weakness – its an invitation to meet you there. Hand it to Him. He can carry it all. He can redeem what feels wasted. He brings comfort with His transforming love.

Matthew 11:28 " Come to Me, all you who are weary and burdened, and I will give you rest."

- **The Path of Holding On:** Keep clutching the hurt, and it will grow into resentment, self-blame, or despair. The weight only increases the longer you hold it. You will begin to live with toxic life patterns. (More injustices, more pain…) and the cycle repeats until you reach that crossroad again and choose the path of surrendering it all to Christ.

Friend, you don't have to carry this alone. The Good Shepherd walks with you, even through the valley. He does not promise to erase the ache instantly, but He does promise His presence—and that makes all the difference.

Framework for Reflection

Name the Wound

- What hurt you?
- What felt unfair, painful, or confusing?

※ "Lord, I bring to You the pain of ____. I don't want to carry this alone anymore."

Recognize the Loss

- What has been taken, changed, or ended?
- Is there something you grieve that others didn't see?

※ "Jesus, I acknowledge this loss. Walk with me as I let go of what I can't change."

Ask for His Presence

- Where do you need His comfort, guidance, or clarity?
- Are there lies you've believed that need to be replaced with truth?

※ "Lord, meet me in this place. Help me see what You see. Heal what I cannot heal on my own."

Release Bitterness, Receive Healing

- Are there people or situations you need help forgiving?
- What do you want to surrender?

※ "I choose to forgive, even if I don't feel it yet. Jesus, give me Your strength to release what poisons me and to receive Your peace instead."

Claim the Growth and Redemption

- How have you grown through these trials?
- Where do you see signs of resurrection — new life after loss?
- God does not erase the past, but He can redeem it — restoring dignity, voice, and wholeness.

�֎ "Lord, turn this pain into purpose. Heal what was broken. Use what was meant for harm and make it part of my testimony. Continue shaping me into someone who reflects Your love."

"He has sent Me to bind up the brokenhearted, to proclaim freedom for the captives... to comfort all who mourn... to bestow on them a crown of beauty instead of ashes."
— Isaiah 61:1–3

You Are Not Alone

Jesus doesn't promise to remove all hardship, but He promises never to abandon us in it. That's the path of healing: not escape, but companionship with the Healer.

Psalm 23:4 "Even though I walk through the valley of the shadow of death, I will fear no evil, for You are with me..."

Re-Entry Is A Process, Not An Event

THE IMPORTANCE OF DEBRIEFING

Coming home is not just about unpacking your suitcases—it's about unpacking your soul. That's why debriefing is essential. It helps you finish one chapter well so you can step into the next with freedom.

Think of your journey as a book with two parts: the years you lived and served abroad, and the season of returning home. Debriefing is like placing a bookmark at the end of one story and opening the page to the next. Without it, you risk carrying unresolved hurt, confusion, or even guilt into the new season.

Why Debrief Twice?

- Before Leaving the Field: Taking time to reflect while still in context gives you clarity. You can process the highs and lows while the memories are still vivid, and you can begin to let go in a healthy way.
- After Returning Home: Once you're back, unexpected emotions often rise—reverse culture shock, grief, even anger. Debriefing again in your passport country gives you space to process these fresh feelings and to begin healing.

What Debriefing Can Do

- Helps you recognize growth as well as grief.
- Gives you language to express what you've been through.
- Allows you to release bitterness and disappointment before they take root.

- Affirms that your story has value—and that God is still writing it.

Don't see debriefing as optional. See it as a gift. Whether through a trusted friend, a pastor, a counselor, or a missions care worker, give yourself the gift of telling your story in full, in the presence of someone who will truly listen.

Debriefing is essential for walking forward with freedom

POSITIVE STEPS FOR A HEALTHY RE-ENTRY

Returning to your passport country can be just as life-shaping as your years overseas. Here are some gentle but practical ways to walk this road well:

Stay Anchored in God

Make space for Him daily. Keep prayer, Scripture, and worship as your lifeline—just as you did on the field. He hasn't changed, even though everything else seems to have.

Journal the Journey

Write down what you feel, what you miss, and what you notice. Don't edit yourself—be honest. Journaling can reveal patterns, release emotions, and help you see God's hand even in the confusing moments.

Lean on Trusted Relationships

Find one or two people who "get it"—friends with cross-cultural experience, fellow missionaries, or compassionate listeners. Let them walk beside you in this transition.

Protect Your Energy

It's tempting to hit the ground running, speaking at churches, visiting supporters, and saying yes to every invitation. Build in margin:

- Rest: Take a day or two simply to breathe and be.
- Exercise: Move your body in ways that refresh you.

- Fun: Allow yourself to laugh and enjoy life at home.
- Connection: Schedule intentional time with the people who matter most.

Bring a Piece of "There" with You

Keep a few mementos from your host culture—a woven cloth, a favorite recipe, a photo. These touchstones can remind you of God's faithfulness and help you integrate your past into your present.

Allow Yourself to Grieve

Re-entry means loss: of people, of place, of purpose. Don't rush through grief or hide it. Jesus Himself wept at loss. Grieve honestly, and let Him meet you in it.

Reframe the Experience

Instead of asking, "Why can't I go back?" ask, "Lord, how will You use what I learned there in this new season?" Reframing shifts your focus from what's gone to what God can redeem.

Seek Support if Needed

If you find yourself sinking into prolonged sadness, anger, or isolation, don't hesitate to seek professional help—preferably from someone familiar with missions and re-entry. It's not weakness to ask for help. It's wisdom.

Embrace the "New You"

The person who left is not the same person who has returned. That's not failure—it's growth. Welcome the changes God has worked in you. Let His Spirit continue to shape you into someone who can serve and love in fresh ways, right where He has placed you now.

Re-entry is not about "going back." It's about moving forward. You are not returning to who you were—you are stepping into who you are becoming. Let the Lord carry your griefs, redeem your story, and use your experiences for His glory in this next chapter.

SECTION 3

SUPPORTING
THE ADVENTURERS

The following thoughts and ideas are relevant for adventurers as they transition back home, as well as for the support team that walk along side them. Both groups play an important role in the re-entry process: Adventurers carry the experiences and stories of their time abroad, while supporters provide the listening ear, encouragement, and practical care that make the journey home more sustainable. These insights are meant to guide both sides.

CARING FOR ADVENTURERS DURING RE-ENTRY

Be a Safe Support

Re-entry can be overwhelming. Many missionaries quietly wonder, "Who can I process this with?" They need a safe listener—not a fixer. Be a guide to their home culture and help with nitty-gritty details like:

- Kids & School: The soccer sign-ups are online now, or everyone's talking about apps your kids have never used.

- Microwaves, washing machines, even smart thermostats can feel like alien technology after years overseas.

- Every day errands suddenly feel like navigating a complicated maze. Scheduling a doctor's appointment, finding a reliable dentist, or figuring out health insurance can feel completely overwhelming.

The "small" things often feel huge. Your patient, judgment-free support helps them re-orient.

Be Present in This Season

Re-entry isn't the end of their journey—it's the start of a new (and often disorienting) chapter. Show up in practical and relational ways:

- Thank them for their service and sacrifice.
- Celebrate them—whether through coffee, dinner, or a simple welcome-home gathering.
- Acknowledge the mix of loss, transition, and growth they're experiencing all at once.

Keep Showing Up

Re-entry takes time. One conversation won't be enough. Keep checking in—at 1 month, 3 months, 6 months, even a year later. Ask with sincerity, "How are you—really?" Consistent presence reminds them they're not alone in the process.

WHAT IS MY PART AS A SUPPORTER?

Your role is to be a guide, a listening ear, and a source of practical help—reminding them they're not alone, no matter how isolating the re-entry process can sometimes feel.

- **Be Available:** Sometimes, just being a constant presence is enough. Reach out to them regularly, offering support without being overwhelming. Sometimes a simple "How are you really doing?" goes a long way.
- **Be Patient:** Re-entry isn't linear, and they may feel up one day and down the next. Allow them to process at their own pace without rushing the healing process.
- **Provide Resources:** Point them toward helpful resources, like support groups, online forums for missionaries, or professional counseling if they need it. There's no shame in seeking professional help during re-entry.
- **Encourage Small Wins:** Recognize and celebrate even small steps in their reintegration. Whether it's adjusting to new routines or feeling a sense of peace in their new reality, small victories matter.
- **Help with Practical Matters:** As mentioned, offer assistance with logistics—whether it's finding a new place to live, navigating healthcare, or understanding changes in their home country. This will free them up to focus on their emotional and spiritual healing.

Practical Examples of Support

Emotional Support & Understanding

- **Need:** Missionaries often feel misunderstood or disconnected from those back home. The return can stir a mix of emotions like grief, guilt, or confusion.
- **Your Role:** Listen actively. Validate their feelings without judgment. Be a safe space where they can express their frustrations, sadness, or excitement about the transition.

Acknowledge Reverse Culture Shock

- **Need:** Re-entry is often more challenging than people expect due to "reverse culture shock" — the disorientation felt when adapting to a familiar culture that feels unfamiliar.
- **Your Role:** Acknowledge the struggle and remind them that their feelings are normal. Offer empathy and let them know they're not alone in feeling this way. Share that adjustment takes time and can be unpredictable.

A Chance to Process the Experience

- **Need:** There's often a lot to process after being immersed in a different culture for an extended time. They need space to reflect on their journey.
- **Your Role:** Encourage debriefing sessions. Provide a space for them to reflect on their experience and share what they've learned and how they've grown. If you can, help facilitate these conversations or point them to a counselor or mentor who specializes in re-entry.

Support in Reintegrating (Emotionally and Practically)

- **Need:** Coming back home isn't just an emotional shift—it often involves practical adjustments as well, like finding housing, managing finances, and even understanding current technology or cultural shifts.
- **Your Role:** Help them navigate these practical aspects of re-entry. Offer assistance with finding housing, reestablishing routines, or even catching up on what has changed in the world. Your practical help can reduce stress and allow them to focus on healing.

Connection with a Supportive Community

- **Need:** Missionaries often miss the deep connections they formed in their mission field. Coming back to familiar places doesn't always mean they feel reconnected.
- **Your Role:** Encourage them to engage with a supportive community, whether that's a church, a small group, or a team of people who understand the mission experience. Be proactive in connecting them with people who are willing to walk alongside them during this transitional period.

Healing from Loss or Grief

- **Need:** The transition can bring up feelings of grief—not just for the people or place left behind, but also for the sense of purpose that was once so clear.
- **Your Role:** Be patient with their process. Allow them to grieve without rushing them through it. Offer consistent encouragement as they rediscover purpose and meaning in their new chapter.
  If needed, connect them to a counselor who specializes in mission-related trauma or re-entry issues.

Encouragement to Take Time to Adjust

- **Need:** Many missionaries feel pressure to jump back into "normal life" quickly, but re-entry is a slow process.
- **Your Role**: Gently remind them that taking time to adjust is okay. Encourage rest, reflection, and personal care during the transition period. Help them avoid burnout by offering space and avoiding unrealistic expectations.

Re-Entry is a process, not an event.

STRATEGIES FOR CARE

Re-entry can feel like stepping into a new world in a familiar place. These strategies offer practical tools and spiritual guidance to help you walk with adventurers to process, reconnect, and land well—both at home and in their heart. Whether a missionary's assignment was short or long-term, returning home can bring unexpected challenges, moments of grief, and opportunities for growth. As a support team, your role is to provide encouragement, presence, and practical guidance, as they step into this new chapter. Plan debriefing **both** before and after returning to provide practical tools for a smooth transition.

Remind them that the goal is one clear, reachable step, not a whole life plan—something real and doable for the season.

When to Begin

For assignments of 1–5 years, it's helpful to schedule 3–5 transition conversations, beginning 3–6 months before departure. For assignments longer than 5 years, consider starting even earlier—up to 12 months before returning to their passport country. Starting early gives space to process experiences, prepare emotionally and practically, and adjust gradually. The final months often fill quickly, so proactive support ensures a healthy, thoughtful transition.

Navigating the Return:

Reflection and Preparation before Re Entry

There are emotions returning missionaries often cannot fully anticipate—like the quiet ache of feeling unseen or unknown—but thoughtful preparation can help them notice and name these feelings as they arise. As a support team, you can walk alongside them by normalizing the re-entry experience, helping them understand the dynamics of reverse cross-cultural stress, and gently pointing out both how they have changed and how home may have shifted during their absence. You can also help them anticipate potential losses, whether in roles, routines, relationships, or familiar places, providing a compassionate space to reflect and process before they fully arrive.

Encourage reflection on expectations, available support, and companions who can walk closely with them..Listen first, guide gently, and create space for honesty. Check in multiple times—1 month, 3 months, 6 months, and 1 year— to walk alongside them through this ongoing process.

Navigating the Return:

Reflecting on the Journey after Re-Entry

Debriefing gives missionaries the opportunity to "travel lightly"—spiritually, physically, and emotionally—so they can step into the next season with gratitude and perspective. Encourage them to reflect on their time in the field, noticing what stands out and what has shaped them.

Encourage them to map out a highs-and-lows timeline, highlighting key breakthroughs and challenges, reflecting on how their expectations compared with reality, celebrating the successes and fruit of their work, and honestly acknowledging any difficulties or pain along the way.

Help them name areas of personal growth—spiritual, emotional, and relational—and recognize where they have seen God's faithfulness. As a support team, your role is to listen deeply, validate their experiences, and guide the conversation gently, without trying to fix everything, creating space for clarity, understanding, and integration.

Practical Tips: These practices don't solve everything, but they provide structure, support, and space for God's grace during this transition

- Writing an unsent letter to someone or a place can bring release, even if it's never sent.
- Identify 2–3 people who will check in at days 30, 90, and 180, and put those dates on your calendar.
- Establish one small rhythm at home—a daily walk, weekly Sabbath meal,or prayer time—to anchor the first three months. Include intentional routines that nourish your body and soul—exercise, quiet reflection, creative expression, or simply sitting outside each day to reorient your senses.
- Journaling: Each day, write one note of thanks and one note of honest lament to process emotions and honor both joy and struggle.
- Make a short list of key people and send a note, voice message, or small token to express gratitude and closure.
- Choose one achievable, meaningful step each week—like reconnecting with a friend, attending a familiar community event, or completing a practical task at home—to build momentum and confidence.

By weaving these small but intentional practices into daily life, returning missionaries can create space to rest, process, and integrate experiences while receiving the support and grace they need for this season of transition.

Settling Into a Permanent Return

Returning home permanently can bring a swirl of emotions—guilt, unfinished goodbyes, unmet expectations, and lingering conflicts. As a support team, you can walk alongside them by helping them name what feels left undone and offer it to God, acknowledge goals that weren't fully realized while trusting God to meet them there, and address conflicts where possible while accepting that some matters may remain unresolved. Your steady presence, encouragement, and gentle listening create space for them to enter this new chapter with honesty, humility, and a sense of peace, knowing they are not navigating it alone.

Re-Entry Conversation Guide

Practical & Logistical

- What plans are already in place for your return?
- What pieces still feel unsettled or unclear?
- Which daily tasks feel most overwhelming or unfamiliar?
- How will you handle housing, transportation, or schooling for children?
- What routines or habits from your assignment do you want to maintain?

Relational & Community

- Who can you talk to who truly understands your experience?
- What relationships are you most looking forward to re-engaging with?
- Are there relationships that feel strained or distant?
- How do you anticipate reconnecting with family, friends, or church?
- What social support would be most helpful?

Emotional & Identity

- How have you changed since your assignment? How has home changed?
- Which parts of returning feel exciting? Which feel intimidating?
- What losses—roles, routines, or relationships—are you noticing?
- How will you know if re-entry is going well?
- What fears or anxieties do you have about returning?

Spiritual & Reflective

- How do you understand "re-entry" and "re-entry stress"?
- What is God asking of you in this season?
- How can prayer, Scripture, or spiritual practices support your transition?

- What has God taught you abroad that you want to carry forward?
- How can your experiences deepen your ministry or service at home?

Integration & Moving Forward

- What do you need to let go of to move forward gracefully?
- How will you celebrate accomplishments and lessons learned?
- What is one small, reachable step you can take in the first 30 days?
- How can you maintain perspective and humility as you reintegrate?
- What support structures or habits will help you stay healthy emotionally, relationally, and spiritually?

RE-ENTRY DEBRIEFING GUIDE

Accomplishments

Reflect on meaningful achievements—not just externally rewarded ones, but personal victories as well.

Possible Prompts:

- What have you done in the past year (or period) that you're proud of?
- What strengths or values did you lean on to accomplish those things?

Disappointments and Pains

Without glorifying suffering, name the hard things honestly.

Possible Prompts:

- What didn't go the way you hoped? What felt like a failure?
- Where did you feel let down—by others, by systems, or by yourself?
- Where did you feel misunderstood or unsupported?
- Did you experience physical or mental health struggles?

Griefs and Losses

Loss isn't always about death. It can also include identity shifts, disconnection, or letting go of dreams.

Possible Prompts:

- What have you had to let go of, willingly or unwillingly?
- Were there losses that others didn't recognize or validate?
- What kind of support did you wish for?

Challenges and Growth

Growth often emerges from tension, risk, or discomfort.

Possible Prompts:

- What challenged you the most?
- What did you learn about yourself that you didn't know before?
- What new capacity or perspective have you developed?
- How did you take accountability for something, and the result was growth in your personal life?
- What new challenges caused you to become more resilient or compassionate?

Injustices

Injustice is when something is not just, not fair — not in line with the dignity you were created with. Many people hesitate to name injustices, but healing can't begin where truth is denied. And God Himself is a God of truth, justice, and compassion. You Are Seen. You Are Valued. You Are Held.

God sees every injustice. He weeps with you, and He also rises to act with mercy, truth, and restoration. His justice is not vengeance — it's making things right, beginning in your own heart.

Possible Prompts:

- Were there any situations where you were treated unfairly or harmed?
- Was your voice silenced or your experience dismissed?
- How did power, identity, or bias play a role?

978 1 9 4 5 4 2 3 7 4 1